Treasury of Illustrated Classics™
The Adventures of
Pinocchio
GIANT COLORING BOOK

Modern Publishing
A Division of Unisystems, Inc.
New York, New York 10022

Printed in the U.S.A.
Series UPC: 49180

Mr. Cherry was a carpenter.

Mr. Cherry needed one more leg to make a table.
Just as his axe was about to hit the wood, Mr. Cherry
stopped short. He heard a voice coming from the wood!

Mr. Cherry searched high and low to find where this voice could have come from. "A talking piece of wood could not be," he said to himself.

When Mr. Cherry picked up the wood, it laughed and said, "You're tickling me!"

Geppetto, the good old woodcarver, went to Mr.
Cherry's shop. He was looking for a piece of wood to
make a puppet.

Mr. Cherry gave the talking wood to Geppetto. But he didn't tell Geppetto how unusual it was!

Geppetto was poor and lived in a simple home
that only had one room. He always wanted a son.

Geppetto soon went to work. He wanted to make a puppet that could dance and sing! He decided to name the puppet Pinocchio.

Geppetto put a nose on Pinocchio and it grew longer!
He put a mouth on Pinocchio and the puppet stuck
his tongue out!

Even though he was shocked, Geppetto continued to work hard. He put arms and legs on Pinocchio.

Then, before he knew it, Pinocchio ran out of the
house and escaped!

Geppetto was angry at the naughty puppet. The townspeople thought Geppetto would hurt Pinocchio, so Geppetto was sent to jail!

Pinocchio was happy to be free from his new papa!
When he returned home, he heard, "Cric, cric, cric,"
from a Talking Cricket!

The Talking Cricket tried to warn Pinocchio to be good. But Pinocchio had enough of being lectured.

Pinocchio was very hungry! He asked a neighbor for food. The neighbor poured a bucket of water on the poor puppet's head!

Pinocchio missed Geppetto so much that he cried
himself to sleep. Pinocchio heard a knock at the
door, but he could not get up. He had burned his
feet on the hot coals!

Angry Geppetto came in through the window. But when he saw Pinocchio crying, his anger melted away.

Pinocchio promised to be good and go to school.
Geppetto made his son a paper shirt, shoes from tree
bark and a dough hat. He even sold his own jacket
so Pinocchio could have a spelling book!

On the way to his first day of school, Pinocchio heard music coming from the Great Puppet Theater. Pinocchio decided to sell his spelling book to get in!

To Pinocchio's surprise, the puppets on stage recognized him! They stopped the play to greet their wooden friend.

The fun did not last for long! In walked the
manager, Fire-eater, who had a voice that made
grown men tremble!

Fire-eater was going to use Pinocchio as wood for his fire. But once he heard Pinocchio cry for his papa, he started sneezing.

Fire-eater decided to use Harlequin for his fire
instead, but Pinocchio saved his friend. Fire-eater
was touched. He freed Pinocchio and gave him
five gold coins.

Pinocchio was on his way home to give his papa the coins. But instead of running home, he stopped to talk to a lame Fox and a blind Cat.

After Pinocchio told his new friends about the coins,
they told Pinocchio about Fools Town and the Field
of Riches. Pinocchio went with them instead of
being good and going home to Geppetto.

They stopped at an inn for a meal and a nap. The Cat and the Fox left without Pinocchio. Pinocchio had to pay for the rooms and the meals.

The innkeeper told Pinocchio that his "friends" would meet him at the Field of Riches.

On his way to the Field of Riches, Pinocchio saw the
Ghost of the Talking Cricket. He tried to warn
Pinocchio of danger, but Pinocchio would not listen!

Minutes later, Pinocchio turned around and saw two
thieves in black sacks. Pinocchio put the gold coins
in his mouth and ran for his life!

Pinocchio ran for the entire night. He came to a
house and begged the girl who lived there to open
the door. But it was too late!

The thieves tied Pinocchio to a tree. The little girl, who was really a Fairy, sent a poodle and a falcon to save Pinocchio.

The Fairy called in three doctors to help Pinocchio.
Pinocchio felt sorry for being so disobedient.
He would do anything to get better.

The Fairy gave Pinocchio a glass of water and some medicine. He promised to take the medicine after he had a lump of sugar.

When the Fairy asked where Pinocchio was hiding
the gold coins, Pinocchio lied!

"Your lie has caused your nose to grow long!" the
Fairy chuckled.

The Fairy let Pinocchio suffer for half the day to teach him a lesson. Finally, she called woodpeckers to fix Pinocchio's nose.

The Fairy told Pinocchio that Geppetto was coming.
Pinocchio ran to meet his papa, but instead of
Geppetto, he ran into his two naughty friends.

The Cat and the Fox took Pinocchio straight to the Field of Riches. They made him dig a hole, put the coins in it and cover the hole with dirt.

Pinocchio went to the river for some water. "In twenty minutes," the Fox said, "you'll find a plant with its branches filled with money!"

Pinocchio came back in twenty minutes, but the money was gone! A parrot told Pinocchio that his so-called friends took the money and left.

Pinocchio ran to Fools Town to tell a judge about
the thieves! Instead of punishing the Fox and the
Cat, the judge ordered that Pinocchio be put in prison!

When Pinocchio was finally freed from prison, he headed back to the Fairy's house. "Ouch!" Pinocchio yelled. His leg was caught in a trap!

An angry farmer accused Pinocchio of being a
chicken thief. "As punishment, you'll be my
watchdog tonight," the angry farmer said.

Pinocchio caught the real chicken thieves and saved the day! The farmer set him free.

Pinocchio ran to the Fairy's house. But instead of a house, there was a gravestone in its place.

Suddenly a pigeon appeared. He told Pinocchio
that he had seen Geppetto.

The pigeon dropped Pinocchio in the ocean
to find Geppetto.

The puppet swam for days. A dolphin told him that
a shark might have eaten his papa!

Sad Pinocchio swam until he reached land. Then he walked to a village. In exchange for food, Pinocchio helped an old woman carry water.

The old woman was really the Fairy!

Pinocchio promised to go to school and to be good.
The Fairy said that if he kept his promise, she would
make him a real boy!

Pinocchio went to school every day. He was very smart. The Fairy told him to ignore the bad boys in school. Pinocchio obeyed.

One day, the bad boys convinced Pinocchio to go to the ocean to see the shark. They were jealous of how smart Pinocchio was and started throwing books at him.

One of the books hit Pinocchio's friend Eugene.
Although Pinocchio was not the one who threw it,
he was arrested. Pinocchio ran from the police!

The police dog, Alidoro, was afraid of water. Pinocchio felt bad and helped the frightened dog. Alidoro promised to repay Pinocchio some day.

Pinocchio kept swimming in the ocean. Out
of nowhere, a huge net caught Pinocchio and with
hundreds of fish he was hauled out of the water.

The fisherman was very mean. Pinocchio cried
for his life. Alidoro ran into the cave and
saved Pinocchio.

Pinocchio ran back to the Fairy's house. A snail said he would come to open the door, but it took him hours. Pinocchio kicked the door and his foot got stuck!

The snail gave Pinocchio some food from the Fairy.
The bread was made of plaster. The food was fake.
Poor, poor Pinocchio!

For one whole year, Pinocchio was very good!
"Tomorrow," the Fairy said, "you will become a boy!"

Pinocchio invited his friends to celebrate his becoming a boy. Even his naughty friend Candlewick was invited!

Candlewick was waiting for the coach to Funville.
"It's the best place for boys," Candlewick said. "Why
don't you come with me?"

The boys heard the sound of trumpets and laughing.
The coach to Funville was coming!

Pinocchio decided to go to Funville, too. Funville
sounded much more exciting than school.

Funville was filled with everything a boy could want!
But nothing is ever what it seems!

One day, Pinocchio woke up and looked in the mirror. He had grown donkey ears overnight!

He ran to Candlewick's house. Candlewick was
suffering from donkey fever, too!

The coachman was really a wicked man. His plan from the start was to turn the boys into donkeys.

He sold Candlewick to a peasant and Pinocchio to the circus.

Working for the circus was tough.
Pinocchio had to eat hay.

Pinocchio learned how to dance, stand on his hind legs and jump through hoops.

The opening day of the circus had arrived.
Pinocchio was afraid.

Pinocchio recognized a face in the audience. It was
the Fairy! But poor Pinocchio could not talk anymore.

When Pinocchio tried to jump through the hoop, his leg got caught. He was now disabled.

The ringmaster sold Pinocchio. The buyer wanted the donkey skin to make a drum. He put Pinocchio in the water. But, when he pulled on the rope, he saw a puppet instead of a donkey!

The Fairy had saved Pinocchio again by sending a school of fish to eat the donkey skin. Pinocchio saw a goat in the middle of the sea. He was sure it was the Fairy, so he swam as fast as he could.

He almost made it to the goat, when a huge wave
came. A shark swallowed Pinocchio!
"Escape if you can," a tuna said.

Pinocchio walked toward a light and saw his papa!
Geppetto had been in the shark for many days.

Pinocchio and Geppetto walked to the mouth
of the shark.

Geppetto could not swim, so Pinocchio carried
him on his back. They escaped!

On their way home, Pinocchio and Geppetto saw the Fox and the Cat. The thieves were beggars now. The Fox was really lame and the Cat was really blind now, instead of just pretending to be, as they did before.

Geppetto was very sick. The Talking Cricket told Pinocchio about a farmer who could give him one coin a day if Pinocchio worked for him.

For five months, Pinocchio worked every day! He
even saved enough money to buy Geppetto a coat.

The snail told Pinocchio that the Fairy was very ill
and could not buy food. Pinocchio gave the money
he had saved to the snail for his beloved Fairy.

Pinocchio was rewarded for his good heart!
The next day, he woke up to a new home. Geppetto
was well and the Fairy had turned Pinocchio
into a real, live boy!